Writing in Irish Today

by DAVID GREENE

Published for
The Cultural Relations Committee
of Ireland
by the Mercier Press,
4 Bridge Street, Cork.

41766

SBN 85342 282 6
FIRST EDITION
1972

THE aim of this series is to give a broad, informed survey of Irish Life and culture, past and present. Each writer is left free to deal with his subject in his own way, and the views expressed are not necessarily those of the Committee. The general editor of the series is Caoimhín Ó Danachair.

David Greene is a recognised authority on the Irish language and its literature. He has been, successively, lexicographer to the Royal Irish Academy's Irish Dictionary, Assistant Librarian in the National Library, Assistant Professor in the Dublin Institute for Advanced Studies, and, later, Professor in the same institute. He became Professor of Irish in Trinity College, Dublin, in 1955; in 1967 he returned to the Institute for Advanced Studies as Senior Professor.

PRINTED IN THE REPUBLIC OF IRELAND BY
LEINSTER LEADER LIMITED, NAAS, CO. KILDARE

XVIII

WRITING IN IRISH TODAY

Nua-Litríocht na Gaeilge

DAITHÍ Ó hUAITHNE
do scríobh

Arna chur amach do
Chomhar Cultúra Éireann

ag Cló Mercier,
4 Sráid an Droichid, Corcaigh.

WRITING IN IRISH TODAY

WHEN the Christian missionaries arrived in Ireland in the fifth century, they were confronted by a society which was technically illiterate, but which possessed traditions of great antiquity preserved in formulae which may go all the way back to the shadowy days of the unity of the Indo-European peoples. The name for this body of tradition was the *senchas*, which derives from the same root as Latin *senex* and simply means what is old, and therefore to be honoured; it is an amalgam of what we would now divide into categories such as law, religion, history, genealogy and literature—the first five books of the Old Testament are the nearest parallel familiar to the modern reader. The *senchas* was transmitted 'by the joint memory of the elders, by the passing from one ear to another, by the chanting of the poets', as an eighth-century Irish scholar put it; although the primitive form of writing called *Ogam* had been invented before the coming of Christianity, it was used only for short inscriptions, no doubt magical in purpose, but not for the preservation of the tradition. The church brought the Latin alphabet, hymns in simple metres, and—perhaps most important of all—prose texts in which the truths of religion were set out in ordered style. All these things were innovations, and were probably fiercely resisted at

1

first, but a synthesis between the old and the new learning soon emerged, and the Irish monasteries became the homes of developers of the tradition who bore such ancient titles as that of *fili*, which etymologically means 'seer'; we know that his pre-Christian functions included divination and other forms of magic. The Christian *fili* had given up these functions, and was known as *poeta* when Latin was used, and the equivalence of *fili* and *poeta* or 'poet' has survived into modern Irish. The title *bard*, better known in modern European languages, originally denoted the somewhat lowly member of the learned class who specialised in writing panegyrics; it is this word which survives as the equivalent of 'poet' in Scottish Gaelic and in Welsh. No doubt the *bard* was less esteemed because his economic relationship with the kings and nobles was as clear as that of an advertising firm with a modern corporation, while that of the *fili*, though just as real, was more remote; the whole learned class existed to uphold the status of the landowning aristocracy. We can only guess at what the cultural situation of the masses may have been; it is significant that the vast mass of material relating to Finn, Oisín and the Fianna, which is the common heritage of story-tellers both in Ireland and in Gaelic Scotland, began to penetrate into the official literature only when the Irish monastic system was destroyed in the twelfth century. Even then the new custodians of the tradition still clung

2

to the metres which had been evolved in the sixth and seventh centuries, although we know that song metres already existed and were in use amongst the people.

The Irish poet of the sixteenth century still called himself a *file* (the later spelling of the word), although in fact he lived entirely by selling praise poems to the nobility—that is, by exercising the function which originally belonged to the *bard*. He had retained much of the dignity due to his ancient title and he continued the old ways unchanged; he still composed his poems orally, lying in a darkened room, and his work ended when they had been recited to the patron who might, however, choose to perpetuate them by having them written down in a family poem-book. The *file* still believed that he possessed supernatural powers, and so did the community in which he lived; an agreement between two Irish nobles in 1539 was guaranteed by both the clergy and the poets, thus offering the twin sanctions of excommunication and satirising against the defaulter. (Indeed, no other sanctions could be invoked in a country where the English government had succeeded in preventing the rise of any native central administration, without at the same time extending its own power further than a strip of the east coast.) The reports of Elizabethan travellers and officials attack the 'rhymers' in terms reminiscent of those used by European colonialists about

African witchdoctors, and both Sidney and Shakespeare had heard about their claim that they could rhyme a man to death. To modern eyes the improbability of the claim is heightened by the conventional and pedestrian nature of the verse produced by the poets, which contains nothing shamanistic or magical—or even 'bardic' in the romantic English sense of that word. On the contrary, what is most impressive about it is its extraordinary technical virtuosity; the urbane variations of wellworn themes are expressed in a literary language which had been standardised since the beginning of the thirteenth century and which was the accepted norm over the whole Gaelic-speaking area, which included most of Ireland and the Highlands and Islands of Scotland.

The official poets made poor use of this superb instrument, but fortunately there were other kinds of writing. Both poets and gentry wrote occasional verse, often in modified and simpler forms of the strict metres; much of this has been lost to us, since it was nobody's business to preserve it for posterity, but we have a few score love poems which will stand comparison with anything being written in Europe at the time. Prose writing flourished; to a large extent it consisted of re-working of themes which went back to the *senchas*, but there were also Irish versions of the European romances of the time, and new compositions which combined both elements. At the beginning of the sixteenth century an educated

Irishman had as much to read in his own language as his counterpart anywhere else and all of it, whatever its origins, was racy of the soil, for literal translation was foreign to the tradition. There was no intrinsic reason why Irish literature should not continue to develop and expand.

In fact, it was already doomed by the external political and economic circumstances. Everywhere else the interplay of the printing press and the literate urban class which had invented it was producing a qualitative change in culture; all the towns in Ireland were in the hands of English-speakers and, as the century advanced, so did the spread of the English power. By the beginning of the seventeenth century the country was firmly under English rule and many members of the aristocracy on whom the native culture had depended either adopted English ways or emigrated; the Irish language itself was so much hated by the government that most protestants preferred to see the natives remain catholic rather than offer them the reformed faith in their own language.

Writing in Irish still went on during the seventeenth century; paper was a cheap and welcome replacement for the expensive vellum which had formerly been used, and there were still plenty of people who could write Irish, though there were no longer any schools to teach them. But Irish was now depending on a manuscript tradition at a time when most European languages, even those which had never been written down before, had printed books freely available; even to speak of a manuscript tradition is, in a sense, an exaggeration, for the transmission was largely oral, through the rare manuscripts being read aloud to illiterate audiences. These are not the circumstances in which innovations will appear, and it was a kind of miracle that Geoffrey Keating (died 1645) should have been able to conceive the project of *Foras Feasa ar Éirinn* 'A basis of knowledge about Ireland', which is the nearest thing to a history which the *senchas* had produced. It is, of course, a nostalgic book, written because the author did not wish that all of Ireland and its culture should vanish without record. Keating was still able to use the classical language vigorously and almost without mistakes; so was the somewhat later writer of the *Parliament of Clan Thomas*, a bitter satire on the peasantry who had accepted their new English landlords and showed little regret for the native nobility. By the end of the century, however, the literary language was breaking down and being replaced by the dialects. An extreme example of the rate of decay is afforded by Fr Manus O'Rourke, a Munster priest who lived in Paris in the early years of the eighteenth century, and who had left Ireland without learning to read or write his native language. We have a manuscript by him containing verse in English,

French, Latin and Irish; the compositions in the first three are correct, polished and witty, while the Irish is his native dialect, put down in a barbarous spelling based on that of English with some touches of French. It contains reference to a few popular songs, but we can safely say that the thousand-year old Irish tradition was a closed book to this educated and intelligent man.

During the eighteenth century a handful of devoted men, poor schoolmasters for the most part, maintained a written literature. This consisted partly of the prose tales of the classical period, the relation of which with oral story-telling is one of considerable complexity, and partly of songs in the popular metres which had emerged from obscurity in the previous century. In Munster, at least, the conscious practice of poetry in these song metres became an established custom, and poets gathered together in taverns to exchange their compositions. These poets have been discussed by Daniel Corkery in his book *The Hidden Ireland* (1925), which has had considerable influence in modern Ireland. It is impossible to reject his main thesis, that the history of the seventeenth and eighteenth centuries cannot be written without a knowledge of the culture which sustained the great majority of the population, and was almost entirely oral in character; Corkery, however, makes very sweeping claims for the classical quality of the poetry which it produced. To the modern reader the most outstanding production of the period is *Cúirt an Mheán Oíche* 'The midnight court', written towards the end of the eighteenth century in Co. Clare; in view of the very large number of manuscript copies which survive, as well as its persistence up to recently in the oral tradition, we may safely assume that it was also very popular at the time of its composition. Though traditional in style and colloquial in language, it clearly shows the influence of contemporary English verse in metre and structure and Corkery is reluctant to accept it into the canon constructed by himself, partly because its frank handling of sexual themes offends him, but also because of its obvious break with traditional forms.

Both sexual frankness and foreign themes had long been present in Irish folksong, as has been demonstrated by Seán Ó Tuama in *An Grá in Amhráin na nDaoine* 'Love in the folksongs' (1960), where chapter headings such as 'The Pastourelle' and 'The Chanson d'Amour' indicate the line of argument. These folksongs were consistently ignored by the writers of Irish manuscripts of all periods and they began to be collected and studied only at the end of the eighteenth century, largely by Anglo-Irish antiquarians. The theory of French influence has been generally accepted, but English must have contributed too, for parts of Ireland, including all the old-established towns, have been English-speaking since the thirteenth century, while French was never as influential in Ireland as it was in England. The linguistic evidence also points to a good deal of cultural penetration, in that very ordinary English words which do not connote new ideas are firmly lodged in all the dialects; the fact, for example, that *saghas*, from Eng. *size*, has largely replaced the native *cineál* in the meaning 'kind, sort' must stem from the same sort of linguistic snobbery as makes the English refer to a blind road as a *cul de sac*. In the case of the folksongs, indeed, there is even better evidence of penetration, for Professor de Bhaldraithe has pointed out that the nonsense refrains of songs often contain English sounds foreign to Irish. We may take it that the Munster poets admired by Corkery, while despising the simple folksongs as crude and unmetrical, drew heavily on them for their own more cultivated compositions. They seldom used English themes, however, although most of them knew that language well.

English influence begins to appear more directly in the nineteenth century. The best-known poem of Seán Ó Coileáin, a Cork poet who died in 1817, is nothing more than a translation, in a deliberately archaic style, of an English poem composed by his friend Fr Matthew Horgan. It is sometimes entitled in manuscripts 'The melancholy man's meditations on seeing the Abbey of Timoleague'; the Abbey was, of course, a ruin and it is hardly necessary to say that melancholy and meditations on ruined abbeys

are English rather than Irish in sentiment. Somewhat later, the great John MacHale, catholic archbishop of Tuam from 1834 until his death in 1881,
offered translations from Thomas Moore's *Irish
Melodies*, as well as from the *Iliad*: although he was
a native speaker of Mayo Irish these versions are,
to the modern reader, unbearably stilted and unna-
tural. Yet neither Ó Coileáin nor MacHale was
doing anything very different from what their Welsh
contemporaries were doing; if the written Irish of
today appears less anglicised than modern literary
Welsh, that is because the Irish experiments made no
contact with the illiterate masses and attracted few
imitators. Some interesting innovations remained
concealed in manuscript, such as the diary written
by the schoolmaster Amhlaoibh Ó Súileabháin
between 1827 and 1835, which might be regarded as
the beginning of modern Irish prose-writing were it
not that it was not published until well into the
present century, and so could not serve as a model
for the revivalists. The only printed books which
found their way into the hands of the people in the
nineteenth century were religious, such as Pádraig
Denn's poetry in Munster and Bishop Gallagher's
sermons in Donegal, and it is not on such foundations that a literature is built.

Meanwhile, a popular literature in English was
appearing for the first time. Ireland had already
contributed a great deal to English literature, but

Swift, Congreve and Goldsmith were Irish writers only by accident of birth or residence and made no special appeal to the masses. By the middle of the nineteenth century patriotic journalism such as is associated with the writers of the *Nation* had provided the nucleus of a ballad literature which was to become increasingly important as nationalist agitation of all shades, from O'Connell to the Fenians, poured out propaganda in English. It was no accident that MacHale had chosen Moore's *Irish Melodies* for translation into Irish, for these exercises in nostalgia were the earliest and most classic expression of the genre. As we have seen, they had no effect on Irish literature itself, but patriotic songs in English penetrated even into the Irish-speaking districts; Seosamh Mac Grianna describes a St Patrick's Day procession in his own district where the song was:

This day in the year Irish hearts are uplifted,

And dreams of past glories inspire us to sing . . .
There were in fact no songs of this kind being composed in Irish in the nineteenth century. After the great disaster of the Famine, the Irish-speaking population had, in Petrie's terrible words, forgotten how to sing; they were reduced to the status of a despised minority, most of whom were trying to learn English as fast as they could to fit themselves for the world in which they were living, where not only the foreign church and government, but their own spiritual and political leaders, all took it for

11

granted that English was the only civilised means of expression. By the 1870s Irish was less written, and less read, than at any time in its recorded history and no literary activity worth the name existed.

The movement for the preservation and restoration of the language did not come from the people who spoke it, but from Dublin, and as one element in the great upsurge of national enthusiasm which was to produce an independent Irish state by 1922. Michael Collins, who was one of the chief architects of that state, said that the Gaelic League had been the most important single factor in the movement towards independence. It was the Gaelic League, too, founded in 1893, which called for an Irish literature in Irish as an essential part of its programme for the deanglicisation of Ireland. One aspect of that task was comparatively easy, that is, to publish some of the existing literature, both oral and manuscript; Hyde's *Love Songs of Connacht*, published in the year of the foundation of the League, had an enormous impact on the reading public and was a milestone in the history of Anglo-Irish literature as well as in that of Irish. Not all those interested in Irish, however, regarded this study of the heritage of the past as an unmixed blessing. Fr Peter O'Leary complained in a letter to a friend two years later that Hyde and others had been printing improper songs —possibly because they didn't fully understand them—and that 'these love songs are doing great harm to Irish'. By this he meant that they might turn respectable people against the idea of learning a language which the British establishment was already attempting to dismiss as a worthless peasant patois. Only a few years later Mahaffy, Trinity College's best-known classical scholar, was to tell a government commission that where Irish literature was not religious it was silly and that where it was not silly it was indecent; Mahaffy notoriously knew no Irish, but he was solemnly supported by Atkinson, Trinity's expert on the subject, who went even further in his denigration of the older literature. As W. B. Yeats observed at the time, 'the conditions of Ireland are so peculiar that it is necessary to answer Dr Atkinson lest, as I should imagine, some imperfectly educated priest in some country parish might believe that Irish literature was "abominable" or "indecent". . . and raise a cry against the movement for the preservation of the Irish language'.

This concern for the respectability of Irish literature was felt very keenly by Fr O'Leary himself, as we have seen. Atkinson had in fact stated that 'all folklore is at the bottom abominable' and said plaintively that he had urged Irish speakers to 'translate Robinson Crusoe or something of that kind and let the people have something they can read'. His advice on providing translations of harmless English books was not followed until thirty years later, but O'Leary set to work to provide suitable reading material for the young which—to translate his own words literally—'would be free from the faults which were in the greater part of the language of the poets'; what he had in mind were the references to women and drink which were common in the folksongs as well as in the more cultivated verse of eighteenth century Munster. He was able to find an Irish folklore variation of the universal theme of a man who sells his soul to the devil, which could be appropriately handled in the language and rhythms of his native West Munster; his book, *Séadna*, had an enormous success and established its writer as an authority on all questions relating to style and usage. In doing so, it resolved a problem which had been agitating the early revivalists: in what language was the new literature to be written?

Had Irish had either a continuous literary tradition, or none at all, the problem would have been an easier one. In neighbouring Wales the literary tradition had never completely broken down and the Welsh Bible was always in the hands of at least a part of the population; when Welsh became widely used in writing and print under the impetus of the Nonconformist Revival there could be no question of what norm to adopt, even though some hymn-writers found that only in speech nearer to that of the people could they express themselves fully. In Ireland, on the other hand, dialect had been the normal means of expression for over two hundred years, and only a handful of scholars had a command of the old literary language. But it was there, and the antiquarian work of the nineteenth century had resulted in the editing and publication of some important texts; most relevant here, a reliable edition of a long religious work by Geoffrey Keating had been published in 1890, with a full vocabulary. Many writers who accepted the impossibility of restoring the classical norm felt that their dialect looked more respectable when clothed in the classical orthography, which had the additional advantage of disguising the wide variation in pronunciation which more realistic spelling would have revealed. While it was generally agreed that all questions of usage must be decided by reference to the speech of the people, there was equally general agreement that a common orthography was desirable, and the question was in fact decided by the appearance of Dinneen's *Irish-English Dictionary* in 1904, using an orthography very close to that of the traditional usage.

The weaknesses of this solution did not appear clearly for some time, though everybody who learned Irish found that he had often to learn a number of different words for the same thing; for example, Dinneen listed *oireamhnach*, *feileamhnach* and *fóirsteanach*, which all derive from a common origin and all mean 'fitting, suitable', each belonging to a different dialect area. The question of style still remained; was it necessary that all writing should follow the patterns of living speech? O'Leary maintained that it should, and that a considerable number of locutions common in other languages had no place in Irish; he gives the following advice to those translating from English:

> Read over the English matter carefully. Take all the ideas into your mind. Squeeze the ideas clean from all English *froth*. Be sure that you allow none of that cozy stuff to remain. English is full of it. You must also get rid of everything in the shape of metaphor. Take instead of it the true idea which the metaphor is intended to convey. When you have the ideas cleared completely of foreign matter, put them in the Irish side of your mind, and shape them in the Irish language, just as you would have if they had been your ideas from the start.

This, though written in English, is itself a good example of O'Leary's prose style, and it would fall easily into Irish. It is also in the spirit of the tradition; as has already been said, that tradition always preferred adaptation to translation, of which the protestant New Testament of 1603 is probably the first true example. It was probably healthy advice in the circumstances of the time, since many of those who were trying to write Irish knew the language none too well, and were in effect translating from English whether they meant to or not; even Douglas Hyde was quite capable of producing Irish

16

incomprehensible to the ordinary speaker. But other doctrinal statements by O'Leary make it clear that nothing which the ordinary man did not say was to be permitted. Thus, in an article written in Irish, he insists that a sentence like 'He was answered by a clear silvery voice from the boat' cannot be translated into Irish but must be rendered by the equivalent of 'The man out in the boat spoke'. Somewhat disingenuously, he goes on to say that Irish ornaments are permissible, and quotes from one of the eighteenth-century Munster poets a description of a lady 'whose noble voice is three times sweeter than the fair harp, the voice of the birds, or of pipes' without, however, indicating how such ornaments are to be incorporated in the Hemingwayesque prose he insists on.

It is true that much of the attraction of the Irish language at this period lay in its freedom from tired literary clichés; George Moore compared it to a newly minted coin, beside which English was rubbed and defaced through having passed through too many hands. Whatever truth there may have been in the simile depended precisely on defining the Irish language as the speech of the people and nothing else; the poetical ornaments in eighteenth century songs praised by O'Leary were as outworn and commonplace as anything in English, and it is significant that he ascribed his quotation to the wrong poet. While it would be an exaggeration to say

17

that he had no interest in the long tradition that lay behind the Irish of the nineteenth century, the fact remains that the versions of it which he offered to the modern reader are all transmuted into his own style: *An Craos-Deamhan* (1905), for example, is a highly readable piece of Irish in its own right, but it conveys little idea to the reader of the goliardic *Aislinge Meic Con Glinne* on which it is based, and those who cannot read Middle Irish must still turn to Kuno Meyer's English translation.

O'Leary's great contribution was that his example and doctrine, though never fully accepted, preserved the purity of the language, which could easily have been destroyed by enthusiastic bunglers. If he had been a creative writer, he might have imposed his native dialect as the new literary norm but, although the Swedish folklorist von Sydow proclaimed that *Séadna* was worthy to be placed beside Goethe's *Faust*, and the eminent linguist Bergin was protesting as late as 1927 that it was of considerable literary merit, they remained in a minority; no writer from any other area was prepared to abandon his own dialect for that of West Cork, and it was not from Munster that the next generation of writers came. It was however, a tribute to O'Leary's doctrine that Patrick Pearse, whose influence was of great importance in the early years of this century, mastered the Irish of Connemara well enough to be counted among the three writers whom Máirtín Ó Cadhain has mentioned as having made a significant contribution to modern prose literature.

Pearse is a difficult man to deal with, largely because his political writings, with their insistence on the blood sacrifice, led straight to the Easter Rising of 1916, after which he, with fifteen other leaders, was executed; he is now, like his colleague Connolly, an apotheosised figure whose theories are rarely studied. His literary output in Irish was small—two plays, a few short stories, and a handful of lyrics— and they are no masterpieces, though still fresh and appealing, but he did much during his few years (1903-8) as editor of the Gaelic League's journal, *An Claidheamh Soluis*, to direct the course of writing in Irish. Previous editors had been scholars rather than writers; while Pearse fully accepted the necessity for preserving the purity of the language, he was impatient of the linguistic discussions which passed for literary criticism at this period. He was deeply read in early Irish literature, and knew that there had been a time when Irish was spoken by princes and poets as well as by peasants; he dreamed of an Irish which would be noble and dignified, not merely indigenous. As Professor John Kelleher was first to point out, Pearse, together with many of the revivalists, was much influenced by Matthew Arnold, and he did not find 'criticism of life' in folklore or in popular songs; over and over again he insisted that the revival must use peasant speech because that

19

was all that was left, but that there should be no question of confining the future development within such narrow limits—'we want no Gothic revival'.

We know that it was the teaching and example of Pearse which influenced the development of Pádraic Ó Conaire (1883-1928), who was better equipped than Pearse for the task of founding a literature which, while using the language of the people, would 'cut the rope of traditionalism which was strangling our writers', as he put it himself. Brought up English-speaking in Galway, Ó Conaire had learned Irish in his grandfather's house in Ros Muc while he was still a boy, and therefore mastered the language in a way that Pearse could not hope to do as a visitor from Dublin. He spent the early years of the century as a minor civil servant in London, but had already begun to write his second language in preference to his first, and he came back to Ireland in 1914. Pearse had not been able to take Irish out of a rural, or an idealised, setting and O'Leary and his followers had no wish to do so; Ó Conaire is the first writer to handle the life of a city convincingly. His critical reputation would be a great deal higher than it is if he had not decided, on his return to Ireland, to earn his living by writing Irish; this heroic gesture inevitably drove him into scribbling journalism, school-books and potboilers, and he died in the deepest poverty. He must be judged on his early short stories, which at their best are worthy to be classed with those of O'Connor and Ó Faoláin in English. As Professor de Bhaldraithe has said: 'He performed a miracle for his own time. He succeeded in learning the craft of the short story; he succeeded in liberating himself from the chief faults which were ruining the attempts of the period—lack of structure, verbosity, over-addiction to outworn phrases, and restricted content. He succeeded in writing literature which was modern both in form and content in a language which had hitherto run wild for lack of cultivation'. To this balanced academic judgment we should add the testimony of the young Seosamh Mac Grianna, brought up in one of the most traditionally-minded Irish-speaking districts of Donegal, on his feelings when he first read Ó Conaire as a youth of nineteen: 'it was like the first taste of wine to a man who had not known until then that there was anything but water in the world'. It was Ó Conaire's example which inspired Mac Grianna himself to take up Irish writing, and it may have been Ó Conaire also who set the example for Mac Grianna's elder brother Séamus Ó Grianna (the two brothers chose different official forms for their surname A' Grianna); the latter, under the pen-name Máire, published *Mo Dhá Róisín*, a novel about the Easter Rising, in 1920, two years after Ó Conaire's collection of seven short stories on the same theme.

The government commission at which Mahaffy

and Atkinson had given evidence in 1899 had finally decided that Irish might be admitted to the examination system of the secondary schools, and a great stride forward was taken in 1909 when the National University of Ireland was founded and, after a controversy which convulsed the country, Irish was made a compulsory subject in its matriculation examination. It was this penetration of Irish into the schools which created a new market for books in Irish and immensely increased the reading public, but it had its attendant dangers. One of the books set for the matriculation examination was Ó Conaire's novel *Deoraidheacht*, written in 1910 when he was still living in London, and describing the trials and temptations of a young Irishman in that city; it is by no means a great book, but worthy of mention as the best attempt at the novel which had yet appeared in Irish, as well as an example of how urban themes could be handled in a peasant language. In 1917, however, Fr O'Leary demanded that it should be dropped from the course, saying that it was an immoral book and that he would never have supported the campaign for Irish in the matriculation examination if he had known that it would lead to such abuses as this. The incident, while trivial in itself, showed the pressures which weighed on the writer in Ireland at that time; it was only five years before, in 1912, that the sheets of Joyce's *Dubliners* had been destroyed, after interminable wrangles

22

with printer and publisher.

The establishment of the Irish Free State in 1922, less than thirty years after the founding of the Gaelic League, seemed to open up great prospects for Irish, which was now recognised as the first official language. It was, however, by no means all gain, for much of the energy which had formerly been devoted to the language movement was now devoted to the problems of running the new state. The Irish language had not been revived, for there were fewer people in the Irish-speaking areas than there had been when the League was founded, and the essentially conservative nature of the new administration did not dispose it to consider the revolutionary methods which would have been needed to reverse a trend which had been firmly established for well over a century. The inhabitants of those areas had been illiterate in their own language until the agitation of the Gaelic League had forced the authorities to provide some minimal teaching for them. Even then, they remained largely dependent on their oral tradition and took little interest in what was being published in Dublin; few of them were well enough off to send their children to the secondary schools where, as we have seen, the new literature was now studied.

The question of standards had remained unsettled since the early days of the movement. A number of linguists, including Bergin, had broken with the

Gaelic League on the subject, and, believing that they had in O'Leary a stylist great enough to set the pattern for a literary language, had opted for writing O'Leary's dialect in a rigidly phonetic orthography; to objections that this process, if extended to the other dialects, would provide Irish with half-a-dozen different norms they replied that it would be healthier to reveal the true situation and let the best dialect win out. They fell here into the same trap as the eminent American linguist Robert A. Hall, Jr., whose polemical book *Leave your language alone!* created such a stir a few years ago. To the descriptive linguist all forms which exist in natural speech are equally correct and worthy of interest: the only forms which are wrong are those which a native speaker does not spontaneously generate. But the structure of modern society is not compatible with linguistic anarchy; laws and official regulations must be written in a rigidly defined norm, and an efficient educational system needs uniformity of the medium of instruction. Literature may benefit from diversity, but it can suffer too; few readers like having to consult glossaries in order to understand their native language. All these facts had been understood, and acted on, in European countries where there were emergent languages; to mention only two examples, the literary norms of Serbo-Croat and Norwegian were fixed during the nineteenth century, by the work of individual scholars and, in each of these cases, the dialect spread was at least as great as in Ireland. By the time the Gaelic League was founded, Norwegian and Serbo-Croat were both being used for official and educational purposes, and scholars purporting to offer advice on the future of the Irish language had a duty to make themselves familiar with what was being done in similar circumstances elsewhere.

They preferred to persist in their prejudices. A symposium was initiated in the influential quarterly *Studies* in March, 1923, by a foreigner, the Jesuit father Gustav Lehmacher, who had learned Irish and was rightly appalled that the Irish, who had lost their literary norm three centuries before, seemed unwilling or unable to devise a new one. Five Irish scholars gave their views on the subject, of whom four had nothing new to offer. Archbishop Sheehan was content with the Gaelic League line, saying that the dialects differed widely to the ear, but not to the eye, meaning, of course, that the Dinneen spelling disguised a multitude of variations. Bergin was still an O'Leary man and believed that 'any artificial blend of dialects . . . would be too grotesque, like a mixture of Lowland Scotch and Cockney English'. This ignored the fact that Lowland Scots and Cockney English are now sub-standard forms only because a standard English exists, as well as the fact that the thirteenth century Irish literary language had been built on a very similar range of dialects, as Bergin himself had demonstrated long before. Dr O'Connell, while shocked by some of the applications of the principle of popular speech ('to render into a peasant patois one of Lamb's essays is a proceeding bound to produce ludicrous effects'), was still an O'Leary man too—though O'Leary would have had no hesitation in carving up Lamb on his own principles. O'Rahilly made the one valid point against standardisation when he said that it was dangerous to tamper with a language 'which can do little more than struggle for bare life', but he felt it was only a question of time before one dialect would by general consent have earned the right to be regarded as the standard one, making it clear that he believed that that dialect would be O'Leary's West Munster.

Only one scholar treated Lehmacher with the attention he deserved, and it is highly significant that this was Tomás Ó Máille, professor of Irish in University College, Galway, and himself a native speaker from Connemara who, unlike the other theorists, was in the habit of using the language daily. The idea of an artificial norm did not frighten him:

> There is bound to be some artificiality about any standard evolved from an earlier literary form, or from the dialects. But language itself is, in the first place, an artificial device which, in the course of time, becomes part of the thinking process and then seems quite spontaneous and

'natural'. Standard German is an artificial language to a large number of the population of Germany. A similar state of affairs to a less degree holds in France. In the case of Irish a standard language would be just as easy or even easier for learners of Irish than learning bits of various dialects or a more or less imperfect form of one dialect as they do at present. As regards native speakers of Irish, the adoption of a few new forms, words and phrases would not be anything beyond them, as we have seen in several instances. In fact, native speakers possessed of a fair amount of culture very willingly adopt such words and phrases when they believe it makes for self-improvement. *Non-native speakers are much more conservative of what they have learned than are native speakers of what they know from childhood.*

The final sentence was italicised by Ó Máille himself, and it proved all too true. Attempts were made to impose the West Munster dialect as the official standard; the Irish version of the constitution of the Irish Free State is, indeed, an example of the use of this dialect for official purposes which showed clearly how adaptable it was, and would have rejoiced the heart of O'Leary himself. But the Irish-speaking area of West Munster was shrinking faster than its counterparts in Connacht and Ulster; furthermore, it was from these latter provinces that the new writers were beginning to appear, writers who were just as proud of their native speech as any Munsterman. The experiment was doomed to failure, and was gradually dropped in favour of the old Gaelic League policy as set out by Archbishop Sheehan; when the enlarged edition of Dinneen's dictionary appeared in 1927, subsidised by a grant from the Free State government, the orthography was, in the editor's words, 'practically identical with that employed in the first edition'. The practical result of this was that, while Irish was now recognised as the first of the two official languages of the state, and was taught in all the schools of the country, it had an orthographical standard, but no norm of grammar, vocabulary or pronunciation. Even that orthographical standard was not fully recognised; emboldened by the Munster experiments in phonetic spelling, writers from other provinces introduced their own variations according to taste.

This did not make the task of the learners easier, and it had unforseen repercussions in the Irish-speaking districts themselves. In his contribution to the symposium mentioned above O'Rahilly had said:

> We have to-day little more than half-a-million native speakers of Irish in Ireland, and (a fact which detracts very considerably from the value of even this small number) all of them save a few thousand old people are speakers of English too. Indeed it is a moot point whether most of

28

the half-million do not know English better than Irish; certain it is that many of our bilingual population speak English habitually and by preference.

His estimate of the number of native speakers was almost certainly too high, but his conclusion was all too accurate. A point which he did not mention was that all but a handful of the total were literate only in English and were totally cut off from reading matter in Irish, unless it could be read aloud to them in the old style. No attempt was made to rectify this as far as the adult population was concerned; the children in Irish-speaking areas were taught through the medium of Irish from 1923 onwards, but in an Irish which, as we have seen, had a wide diversity of norms. For centuries the people had had the innate superiority of the English language proclaimed to them by the English administration and, for more than a century now, by their own religious and political leaders; those who still spoke Irish did not read books at all, but were accustomed to the use of English so as to follow local and national affairs in the newspapers, and to deal with those in authority. The newspapers, local and national, continued to appear in English, and the bewildering variations of the Irish used by government agencies did little to convince the people of the superiority of Irish as an official language; that literacy of the common people which has been the great strength of Welsh failed to develop in Ireland. Nor did well-meant schemes for offering Irish-speaking children better educational opportunities than their English-speaking contemporaries achieve what they set out to do; they produced a class of educated native speakers of Irish such as had not existed for centuries, but which inevitably looked for suitable employment outside their economically distressed rural areas. It is on this class that modern Irish literature depends, but most of its members are now living in English-speaking urban areas, especially Dublin.

The official encouragement of literature was no better conceived than the linguistic policy. It grew out of an entirely praiseworthy effort to provide the large number of school text-books required by the introduction of Irish as a compulsory school subject; by 1928, the *Gúm*, as the governmental publishing agency was called, had decided to turn its attention to literature, offering a fixed rate per thousand words. This was the very year in which Pádraic Ó Conaire died in poverty, and it was plain that some sort of subsidy would be necessary if full-time writers were to exist and if Irish literature was to develop naturally; economic circumstances made the writing of a novel as risky for the author as its publication was for the publisher, and the forms of writing hitherto had been largely shaped by the fact that periodicals were the main medium. But many obstacles confronted the writer who hoped to be accepted by the *Gúm*.

30

Establishment attitudes of the time were fiercely puritanical; the Censorship of Publications Act passed in the same year, 1928, resulted in the banning of most of the work of contemporary Anglo-Irish writers, and it was clear that editors who were civil servants would be just as zealous as O'Leary had been to see to it that nothing would be published in Irish which could not be permitted in English; sexual themes were therefore untouchable. Politics was just as dangerous; the country was recovering from a debilitating civil war which made all recent Irish history too hot a subject to handle. Religion could be treated only in conventional terms; in a state which was 93% catholic from the beginning, any kind of anti-clericalism, real or suspected, was unwelcome. And, finally, the linguistic quibbling which Pearse had condemned more than twenty years before was reinstated; as fine and sensitive a writer as Mgr Pádraig de Brún used to find his translations from the classics 'corrected' by editors who, like a secret police force, had to find errors in order to justify their own existence.

Some writers managed to live with these conditions, notably Séamus Ó Grianna who, until his death in 1969, poured out scores of volumes, mainly collections of short stories. A recent critic has attempted to rehabilitate this body of work, usually dismissed as suitable fodder for an unimaginative school programme, on the grounds that, while

Ó Grianna's picture of life in Irish-speaking Donegal is highly idealised and unreal, 'his great merit is to have created such a land, so that the traveller crossing its border breathes again each time a familiar air and recognises in each new character a family likeness to those whom he has met before'. Few readers of Irish today, however, wish to make this sentimental journey, and the reputation of Ó Grianna's brother, Seosamh Mac Grianna, stands much higher, although he has only a few creative works to his credit.

Seosamh Mac Grianna, always critical of his own work, found that he could not earn a living without lowering his standards, and he turned to translating. The *Gúm* had taken up the suggestion which Atkinson had made thirty years before, and were commissioning translations of *Robinson Crusoe* and other acceptable material—almost invariably English, since that was the only foreign language known to most of the writers. This policy may perhaps have been theoretically defensible, on the grounds that it provided employment for those capable of writing Irish, and reading matter at a rate greater than original work in Irish could have been produced; a further argument, that it served to increase the flexibility of the language, is less convincing for, as we will see, it was not this kind of writing which served as a pattern for the later development of the literature. However worthy the principles, the administration of the scheme was deplorable; Séamus Ó Grianna describes how he tried to insist on handling only worthwhile material at first, but slipped from compromise to compromise until, in the end, 'I would take any miserable rubbish I got—for a pound per thousand words'. He preferred to settle for his facile short stories, which at least were his own; his brother Seosamh continued to tread the translation mill. During the six years 1932-7 the *Gúm* published no fewer than ten books translated by him, of which two (*Hangman's House* and *Coming Through the Rye*) contained more than 500 pages each and another two (*Ben-Hur* and *Ivanhoe*) more than 600 each. What good these books did the Irish-speaking public—all of whom could have read them in English—is not easy to say; we know, however, what harm they did Seosamh Mac Grianna, for his health broke down and he wrote no more.

Meanwhile an interesting development had been taking place on the Blasket Island off the coast of Kerry, among a population of a couple of hundred people. The Norwegian linguist Marstrander had gone there to study Irish as far back as 1907, precisely because it was so isolated, and he was followed by a steady stream of learners, including English scholars of the standing of Robin Flower, George Thomson and Kenneth Jackson. It was an Irishman, however, Brian Ó Ceallaigh, who convinced an old islandman, Tomás Crithin (Ó Criomhthain in the normalised form), that he should write his own life story. This, needless to say, was a new and strange idea, quite foreign to the highly formalised oral tradition, and it was not until Ó Ceallaigh had translated passages from Loti and Gorky to him that Tomás was ready to believe that the circumstances of his life could be interesting to an outside audience. The book which resulted, *An tOileánach* 'The islandman' (1929), is a triumph of Irish prose; here, at last, is the speech of the people producing results far beyond the power of O'Leary, and it will live as long as the Irish language is read. And yet it could not, in the nature of things, be a pattern for other writers, for Tomás Crithin was not writing for his own people (who found the praise accorded to the book entirely incomprehensible) but for the new Irish reading public of the towns; indeed, in his most quoted sentence he makes it clear that he, like Geoffrey Keating three hundred years before, is seeking to preserve the memory of a way of life which is doomed. The success of the book inspired other islanders notably a young man, Muiris Ó Súilleabháin, who published *Fiche Blian ag Fás* (1933) and an old woman, Peig Sayers, with *Peig* (1939). All these writers were translated into English, and *Twenty years a-growing*, the version by Moya Llewelyn Davies and George Thomson of Ó Súilleabháin's book, was described by E. M. Forster as 'an account of neolithic civilisation from the inside', though George Thomson's description of the Blasket society as 'pre-capitalist' is somewhat nearer the mark. It cannot be doubted that it is the exotic nature of that society to the modern reader which has made this strange flowering the best-known aspect of modern Irish literature; as recently as 1969 J. V. Luce published a scholarly article entitled 'Homeric qualities in the life and literature of the great Blasket island'. Indeed, although the Blasket is now deserted and its former inhabitants have been moved to the mainland, 'Blasket literature' still continues, for the sons of Tomás Crithin and Peig Sayers have both published books which continue the tradition. But the gap between documentary and creative writing was not bridged either by Tomás Crithin or by his successors; much had been hoped for from Muiris Ó Súilleabháin, but he died before his promise could be fulfilled.

Irish prose was greatly developed during the twenties and thirties, not only by the works mentioned, but by translations by writers who, though under the disadvantage of having learned the language, compensated for this by their intellectual power and firsthand knowledge of literatures other than that of English. Amongst these Mgr Pádraig de Brún and Professor George Thomson were the most prominent; the latter's short introduction to early Greek philosophy is a brilliant example of *haute vulgarisation* in an Irish which is both authentic and limpid. A beginning of the task of giving the

Russian classics to the Irish reader was made by Liam Ó Rinn, with a translation of Turgenev's *Stikhotvorenia v Proz*. Those who have learned the language are seldom capable of producing creative writing, but that they can do valuable work in other fields was demonstrated by Leon Ó Broin's *Parnell* in 1937, the first of a series of distinguished biographical and historical writings to be produced by this author, both in Irish and English. By the end of the thirties Irish prose was a medium in which any theme of modern life could be handled.

Meanwhile verse was at a standstill. This was very distressing to those who looked back on the glorious tradition of Irish poetry, and who saw what Yeats, now at the height of his powers, was achieving for Anglo-Irish literature. Yet, in retrospect, it was a thoroughly healthy state of affairs. Those who have studied minority literatures know how easy it is for a handful of poets to exploit the neglected resources of their native tongue, without thereby making any impact on the linguistic situation; Mistral did not save Provençal, nor did the Lallans poets avert the steady anglicisation of Scottish speech. Prose is the foundation of all modern literatures and the only form readily accessible to all speakers of a language; poetry may be the highest form of expression, but it is also the plaything of the sentimentalist and dilettante. It was not, of course, theoretical considerations of this kind which dictated the emphasis on prose in the twenties and thirties, but simply that the speech of the people could be applied without much difficulty to the prose patterns common in European literature, such as the short story. The gap between the modern short story and the folk tale is considerable, but it can be bridged; the gap between the folk song and the personal lyric is immense, so great indeed that only an intimate knowledge of a culture other than that of the oral tradition is likely to fit a poet for the task. The senior and most distinguished of our living poets, Máirtín Ó Direáin (b. 1910), has recorded that he did not come into contact with poetry, in the modern sense of the word, until he came to work in Dublin in 1937, though he must have heard many folksongs in his home in Aran. Nothing grew directly out of the folk song. In Munster, the highly ornamented metres and traditional themes of the eighteenth century poets were still remembered, and some rather self-conscious 'courts of poetry' existed where compositions in this style were recited. This was in accordance with Corkery's doctrines, which had led him into vehement controversy with Mgr de Brún, who, like Pearse, adopted the speech of the people but had no use for an outworn tradition. The matter was settled by the inability of the poets of the 'courts' to produce anything better than elegant pastiche; the best-known of them, Tadhg Ó Donnchadha, published hundreds of original compositions and innumerable translations, but it is safe to say that nobody reads him now. It is significant that Tomás Tóibín (b. 1920), who was associated with the Cork 'court' in his early days, now writes in a thoroughly modern idiom. In the twenties and thirties, however, experiments in such an idiom were carried out only by those whose knowledge of the language was defective, and they are of purely historical interest.

The Irish literature of today begins with the emergence of the Connacht writers Máirtín Ó Direáin, mentioned above, and Máirtín Ó Cadhain (1906-70). The latter, a native of Cois Fharraige, as the southern seacoast of Connemara is called, had been trained as a school-teacher and, although he had done some translating, he did not taken up writing seriously until he lost his job; he was in his early thirties when his first book of short stories was published in 1939. These, though immature, brought a new style to Irish: the speech of the people, certainly, but used with a richness, not to say obscurity, hitherto unknown. This wealth of language is not deployed in the traditional manner, but is used to furnish a highly organised system of metaphor and simile which would have shocked O'Leary; nor does Ó Cadhain make any effort to avoid the neologisms thrown up by journalism and official documents —indeed, he often uses Irish which would be condemned as 'untraditional' by the purists were it not for the obvious fact that nobody who has yet written the language is so thoroughly part of the folk tradition, so that even Tomás Crithin's style sometimes seems consciously literary by comparison. These two very different writers have one thing in common, however: it was the reading of Gorki which showed them what they should write about, an experience which Máirtín Ó Cadhain described as being like that of Paul on the road to Damascus. He had already published his first book before it happened and, while feeling that he could do much better, lacked an adequate model for developing his work. Nothing could illustrate better how useful an enlightened translation policy could have been; unfortunately, Gorki still remains unavailable in Irish and, indeed, so does most of Russian literature, some excellent translations of Chekhov by Maighréad Nic Mhaicín being an important exception.

Ó Cadhain's development as a writer was interrupted by the sort of accident which befell Gorky himself, as well as most other Russian writers; as a member of the illegal Irish Republican Army, he was interned by the Irish government for the duration of the European hostilities, and his next book did not appear until 1948. Meanwhile Máirtín Ó Direáin had published his first book of poems in 1942—simple personal lyrics, entirely uninfluenced by traditional forms. Strange to say, it was a lecture by Tadhg Ó Donnchadha, the Munster traditionalist, which made him think of verse as a means of expression;

as he says himself, the lecturer would have been greatly distressed if he had known what he was bringing about. Ó Direáin, too, speaks of the lack of models, without making it clear how he solved the problem:

> In matters of form and style we were greatly handicapped by having no proper models, of the kind we needed badly, that is, some authoritative poet attempting to deal with contemporary problems in contemporary style. If our poetry had been at full flood, rather than at an ebb, from, say 1900 onwards, such a poet would have existed and the change would not have appeared so strange when it came; but it did not appear from the work of the poets of that period that they felt either pain or passion. It must be said too, and I am not blaming them for it, that their work did not indicate that they were exploiting the language to its full extent, whatever the reason may have been. We had two choices when we began, to go on using the traditional style which had been squeezed dry long before we were born, or to use the natural power of the language as we knew it. We took the second choice. As Eliot says: *since our concern was speech, and speech impelled us to purify the dialect of the tribe.* So it was with us.

He goes on to deny that he followed the patterns of Eliot or any other English poet, since they were unknown to him when he began writing: 'I had nothing on which to base anything but what I had heard—*the dialect of the tribe*—I had to base the rhythm of my poetry on the natural rhythm of the language . . .'. The latter sentence must be understood in the widest possible sense, for what Ó Direáin has in mind here is not only the rhythm of conversation, but the familiar cadences of folksong; he rejected the somewhat monotonous metre of the songs, but adapted their idiom to his own purposes. As a result, he uses mainly *vers libre*, with repetition prominent but rhyme reserved for an occasional striking effect. This was not the only way in which modern poetry could be written in Irish, for writers deriving from the Munster tradition have demonstrated the possibility of evolving new metrical forms without in any way interfering with natural speech rhythms. But Ó Direáin's example has been very influential, and most modern verse is free of restrictions—a freedom which has been criticised by Ó Cadhain, who says tartly: 'It is much easier to compose a nice harmless lyric of eight lines now and again than to write an essay, a novel or even a short story'.

1942 was an important year for another reason, for it was then that *An Comhchaidreamh*, an association of Irish-speaking university graduates, dissatisfied with the state of Irish periodical literature, founded the monthly *Comhar*, which immediately became the leading organ of the new literature; it was here that much of Ó Direáin's work was published, as well as that of the younger poets who now began to emerge. Six years later the Gaelic League responded to the challenge by issuing its own literary monthly *Feasta*; these two journals between them have carried most of the experimental writing of the modern period. In 1945, Seán Ó hÉigeartaigh and his wife founded the publishing firm of Sáirséal agus Dill, for Irish books only; by insisting on high quality in the material published, and professional standards in book production, they were able to build up a circulation among the reading public which *Comhar* had shown to exist. In 1948 a book club was begun, which was soon able to assure a modest circulation of 3,000 or so to books chosen, and this encouraged other publishers to enter the field. Even more important, in 1952 the government agreed to give aid without strings to books and periodicals published in Irish, thus enabling private firms to compete on something like equal terms with the State publishing organisation, the *Gúm*. This gave a new freedom of expression to writers in a country where the literary censorship, though still remaining on the statute books, was being gradually relaxed in practice —except in the *Gúm*, where civil servants answerable to a minister were not likely to take any risks. The *Gúm* had published Máirtín Ó Cadhain's second book of short stories in 1948, but only after excising

42

An Strainséara, a deeply sympathetic study of a childless woman, which some critics consider Ó Cadhain's most flawless piece of work. It appeared some years later in a collection published by Sáirséal agus Dill, who had already, in 1949, given us Ó Cadhain's only published novel, *Cré na Cille*. Nobody could call this a flawless book; its very structure, that of dialogues between the dead lying in a Cois Fharraige graveyard, is a clumsy one, and some of the 'interludes' with which that dialogue is interspersed are dangerously overwritten. Máire Mhac an tSaoi's judgment on it was written six years after it appeared, and is carefully considered:

> Overweighted, overburdened, too heavy for the thread of story though it is, *Cré na Cille* is the only thing in Irish, apart from *An tOileánach*, that has a weight and importance out of the ordinary. In the presence of a creative talent so undeniable as that of Máirtín Ó Cadhain, the critic has no choice but humility; he can analyse, but he recognises a value which is independent of him. Ó Cadhain's work lives with a life which owes nothing to literary artifice. As Mauriac has Les Landes, so Ó Cadhain has Cois Fharraige. It does not matter whether the picture is realistic. It has its own life. This is no easy writing, or pleasing writing. The place we see is a remote countryside, inhabited by a gloomy, solitary people, but the whole vibrates with a strange

force, the like of which is not to be found in any other Irish writer to-day . . .

The word translated 'Irish' in the last sentence refers to the country, not the language, and the claim is still valid; Ó Cadhain's Cois Fharraige takes its place with Joyce's Dublin, and *Cré na Cille* is the only book by an Irishman which is worthy of comparison with *Ulysses*. Whatever else may be said about the new literature, it can at least be asserted with confidence that the best Irish author of recent times wrote in Irish.

While no such sweeping claims can be made for other writers, progress during the forties and fifties was steady and assured. One encouraging development was the return of Liam O'Flaherty, already well-known as an English writer, to his native language—he is like Ó Direáin, an Aran man (b. 1897); from 1946 onwards he wrote occasional short stories in Irish, and a collection was published in 1953. This volume offered the material for an interesting stylistic analysis, for several of the stories had been published also in English, sometimes in two versions. It becomes clear that, consciously or unconsciously, O'Flaherty follows the doctrine of O'Leary about the difference of style appropriate in Irish and English; thus, a sentence which reads in Irish 'the wisps were kept in the air' reads in one English version 'the wisps were maintained afloat by the sweeping blast' and, in the other, 'they were

44

maintained in the air by the fierce gale. Many will prefer the Irish in this case; it is possible to argue, however, that the simple direct style is appropriate to a man writing his native language without the benefit of a long prose tradition which might serve as a model, and that the same man gratefully avails himself of such a tradition when he turns to another language. The concern of a writer is not only to purify the speech of the tribe, but to enrich it, and it was the great merit of Ó Cadhain that it was the enrichment of the language, if sometimes at the expense of clarity, which was his constant concern.

O'Flaherty's contribution to the new Irish literature has, unfortunately, been only one book; the same is true of Brian O'Nolan (1911-66) who, like O'Flaherty, is better known as an English writer, chiefly by his brilliant fantasy *At Swim-Two-Birds*, first published in 1939 and several times reprinted. During the forties O'Nolan wrote a daily column for the *Irish Times*, alternately in Irish and English, and it is impossible to say how many people were first brought to use the Irish they learned at school by the desire to find out 'what Myles is saying to-day' —'Myles na Gopaleen' and 'Flann O'Brien' were his chief pen-names. The very title of his one book in Irish, *An Béal Bocht* (1941), is hard to translate except by its Hiberno-English equivalent 'the poor mouth'; one who is always complaining about his plight is said to have 'the poor mouth', and the book is a joyful satire on the Blasket and Donegal writers, as well as on the whole establishment of the revival movement.

A third writer who was deeply interested in Irish was Brendan Behan (1923-64); he wrote a few pleasing poems, but by far his greatest contribution was the play *An Giall*, first written and produced in Irish, but known to a wider audience as *The Hostage*, after being translated by the author and adapted by Joan Littlewood.

This is the first time the drama has been mentioned, though plays were being written in Irish from the beginning of the revival movement, when a sketch by Douglas Hyde, *Casadh an tSúgáin* 'The Twisting of the Rope', was played in almost every parish in Ireland. In no country in the world is there more interest in the drama, and amateur theatre festivals are almost as common as *eisteddfodau* in Wales, so that writers find it easy to have their plays produced, though seldom at any great financial profit. Hundreds of plays have been written in Irish, but, in spite of this, the Irish language theatre, Taibhdhearc na Gaillimhe, which was founded in Galway in 1928 had to depend largely on translations and only recently has the Damer theatre in Dublin offered regular productions of original plays. There has never been a shortage of actors or producers— Micheál Mac Liammóir, Cyril Cusack and Siobhán MacKenna, to mention only a few—but no dramatist of importance has emerged. This is perhaps to be expected, for it is hard for dramatists to learn their trade without the existence of a flourishing theatre. During most of the period under review, Ireland was able to maintain only two permanent professional theatres, both of them in Dublin, and as eminent an authority as Micheál Mac Liammóir has recently spoken with pessimism about the future of the professional drama in the country. If this is the case of the English-speaking theatre, with such glories as Synge and O'Casey behind it, the situation for the Irish-speaking theatre is infinitely worse, for it is of necessity centred in Dublin where Irish-speakers interested in the theatre constitute a minority of a minority—only three years ago, the critic of *Feasta*, reviewing a play which had been performed at the Damer, remarked that it was an unusual occasion in that, although the house was nearly full, he recognised only two of the audience! While it must be admitted that it would be just as surprising to recognise only two of the audience at a first night in the Abbey or the Gate, and that the Anglo-Irish drama has no great contemporary figures either, the poverty of the English-speaking theatre in Ireland is of little comfort to those concerned with Irish.

Poetry made rapid advances in this period; by 1950, enough new and interesting material had appeared in the periodicals for Seán Ó Tuama, a young poet and scholar, to produce the anthology

Nuabhéarsaíocht 'New verse', which, in turn, made the movement known to a wider audience. The master was still Máirtín Ó Direáin, whose range of subject and command of language were gradually extended in volumes published in 1943, 1949 and 1957. The last of these, *Ó Morna*, takes its title from the first poem in the book, a powerful and technically assured study of the brutish life of a landlord of pre-Land League days, which incidentally throws a cold light on the 'hard-riding country gentlemen' so frequently praised by Yeats. In the large body of Ó Direáin's work, only a few failures—such as a poor imitation of Ezra Pound—show any influence from foreign models; while we know that he read widely at this time, all his best work is derived, as he claims himself, from the tradition in which he grew up, and which he had expanded immeasurably. Like Ó Cadhain, he has been ready to depart from his native dialect and to borrow new words whenever they seem needed, to the horror of some linguistic purists—I have heard a professor of Irish dismiss one of his lyrics as incomprehensible. But innovations are necessary for the criticism of modern Irish society, which is his main concern; unlike some of his imitators, he has moved steadily away from purely personal themes.

Two important poets made their appearance at this time, both of them deriving from the Munster tradition. Seán Ó Ríordáin was born in the Irish-speaking district of Baile Mhúirne, Co. Cork, in 1917, but has lived most of his life in Cork City. His first book of poems was published in 1952, and immediately awakened considerable interest. He is quite explicitly concerned with moral and philosophical problems; the preface to his book opens with the question 'What is poetry?', which is answered at some length. Such discussions were a novelty; Corkery, whose influence Ó Ríordáin acknowledges in a poem, was mainly concerned with the form and content of verse rather than with metaphysical problems, and Ó Direáin, as we have seen, saw his task as that of purifying and enriching the language he had inherited. Ó Ríordáin's work was warmly greeted by those who had rejected the mindless traditionalism of earlier writers, but wished their literature to be concerned with values as well as with technique. A quite remarkable amount of exegesis was devoted to Ó Ríordáin's small output —he did not publish another book until 1964—and a howl of rage went up when a critic dismissed the content of his work as 'ordinary scruples of conscience disguised in an Irish dress'. This was no doubt too harsh a judgment, but it may be argued that Ó Ríordáin is at his best in such poems as that on the funeral of his mother, which is a simple and deeply moving expression of personal emotion.

Máire Mhac an tSaoi, born in Dublin in 1922, was brought up Irish-speaking by her mother, the sister of Mgr Pádraig de Brún, and she spent much of her childhood in her uncle's house in Dunquin, on the mainland opposite the Blasket Island. Her uncle, whose devoted work as a translator has already been mentioned, had a magnificent command of the language and great talent as a versifier; both of these Máire Mhac an tSaoi also possesses, adding to them a creative talent which he lacked. Her one volume of verse, published in 1956, contains much early work which, while talented, is of no particular importance; it also contains a number of lyrics which surpass anything written in this century—or, indeed, for many centuries before. Outstanding among these is a series of short poems in which a woman reflects on a dying passion; only in Old Irish do we find anything of comparable intensity.

These three poets were singled out for special notice by Valentin Iremonger, himself a distinguished writer in English, in an essay published in 1955, and his example was followed by Frank O'Brien, an American critic, in his survey of modern Irish poetry, *Filíocht Gaeilge na Linne Seo*, published in 1969. While this may be unfair to many other writers—Tomás Tóibín, to name only one, has written a number of fine poems—these were the acknowledged leaders of a period which re-established Irish poetry. Iremonger's judgment is worth quoting:

> By and large, the poetry that appears to-day in Irish magazines is as good as that which appears

in contemporary English and French magazines, and one should beware of looking for more than that. Masterpieces are not produced in a vacuum, and it would be unwise to seek for them in the present stage of Irish writing. But the foundations are being well-laid and, at some stage, the magical accident, as Dylan Thomas called it, will happen.

As will be seen, it cannot yet be claimed that the magical accident has happened in Irish poetry, but it is certain that the foundations were laid at this time, in that poets began to write freely again; if some of them were not worthy of the name, nothing is more certain than that good poetry cannot exist without bad poetry existing as well.

All these works were published in a language which was being slowly standardised, not by writers or scholars, but by civil servants acting on instructions from the government. In the early forties Mr de Valera, then Prime Minister, requested the Translation Section of the staff of the Irish parliament to devise a 'short orthography which it would be suitable to accept as a common standard', and a booklet of 62 pages embodying the results of their work was published in 1945. It was, of course, much more than a spelling reform which was offered; no fewer than 17 pages were taken up by recommended grammatical forms. Most people, including the present writer, found some, at least, of the recommendations distasteful, but most of us gradually came to the conclusion that even a faulty standard was better than none. In 1953 an experimental grammar was published, and criticisms invited; on the basis of these, a revised grammar appeared in 1958. In 1959 an *English-Irish Dictionary*, edited by Professor Tomás de Bhaldraithe, was published officially; the Irish equivalents are given in standardised spelling.

Most books and periodicals now follow the official norm, but there are exceptions. Máirtín Ó Cadhain, who was for some years himself a member of the staff of the Translation Section, published an eloquent attack on it under the title 'Bad luck to these conventions' in an Ulster journal in 1962; it may be said in passing that the Ministry of Education in Northern Ireland had carefully fostered Donegal Irish as the official standard in their schools, and the Dublin norm was felt by many Ulster speakers to have ignored the special features of their dialect —indeed, Séamus Ó Grianna, right up to his death, succeeded in having his books published by the *Gúm* in the Dinneen spelling. He was the only really successful rebel; Ó Cadhain's works appear in an orthography which diverges very little from the norm. The question of vocabulary is still unsolved, and readers have to grapple with a wide diversity of words; de Bhaldraithe's *Dictionary* gives *oiriúnach*, *fóirstineach* and *feiliúnach* as equivalents of 'suitable' and, as noted above (p. 15), these are not words having different ranges of meaning, but simply local variants. To make matters worse, there is still no Irish-English dictionary but the Dinneen of 1927, which, apart from using the old spelling, lists only a fraction of the words brought into writing in the last forty years; Ó Cadhain's first two books, as issued by the *Gúm* for use in schools, each contain up to ninety pages of glossary and linguistic notes. The Department of Education has a staff working on a dictionary which will make the new literature more accessible to the average reader, but it will be several years before it is ready.

The last ten years have, on the whole, been some-what less exciting than those which preceded them. Máirtín Ó Cadhain, who became a lecturer in 1956, published no major work during most of that period; it was not until 1967 that a new volume of short stories appeared, showing that his great talents were still developing, and it was appropriate that this book should be the first to receive the Butler award of £2,000 offered by a generous Irish-American for creative writing in Irish. Shortly before his death he published a lecture given to a gathering of writers in 1969, in which he discussed at length the problems confronting the Irish writer; it would be most desirable to have this available in English, for never before had a writer of such power and achievement spoken so frankly about the situation. It was in this lecture that he said that the trouble with verse at the moment is that the good poets are writing too little and the bad poets too much. With the exception of Máirtín Ó Direáin, this is undoubtedly true; Ó Ríordáin produced one book in the sixties and Máire Mhac an tSaoi only a few poems in periodicals, while none of the younger poets has reached the standard which these three had achieved by their thirties.

After Ó Cadhain, there are few prose writers of interest. One exceptionally hardworking and productive author has, however, already made his mark; Diarmaid Ó Súilleabháin, born in 1932, has experimented freely both with language and style and has published a number of novels. The main criticism of his work has been that it is too ambitious; brought up in an English-speaking environment, he lacks the linguistic resources that enabled Ó Cadhain to adapt traditional speech to modern forms. In the present state of Irish writing, however, Ó Súilleabháin's devotion and tenacity of purpose are not to be despised, and it is encouraging that the Irish Academy of Letters, never particularly concerned with writing in Irish, has recently awarded him a prize for one of his novels.

Indeed, the moribund state of that Academy, founded so hopefully by Yeats, proves better than anything else the need for a literature in Irish, for Anglo-Irish literature has proved to be a myth. Not that Irishmen do not write well in English—or in French, as Beckett has demonstrated—but that they simply become absorbed in the mainstream of English literature; a panel of young Anglo-Irish poets interviewed recently by the *Irish Times* proved quite unable to say what was distinctively Irish in their work. Even Thomas Kinsella, who is deeply interested in the Irish past, and whose translation of the *Táin* is one of the finest books to be produced in Ireland, could not be identified as Irish from his poetry. If Ireland is to speak with an authentic voice, it must be in Irish, and the work of this century has laid the foundations well, as Iremonger said fifteen years ago. But will the magical accident ever happen, and the likes of Yeats and Synge appear in Irish? Or, to be less ambitious, will we ever have as full a cultural life in Irish as other small nations possess —as full as that which Israel has already attained?

A beginning has been made. Apart from creative literature, the volume of historical, biographical and academic writing in Irish has steadily increased and we have arrived at the point when an Irishman who does not read Irish cannot now claim that he is fully abreast of the work being done in these fields. But the total output of books is still pitifully small; a few years ago, an Irishman who knows Iceland well pointed out that in that country, 'with a population less than that of County Cork, the new titles published for the Christmas market each year exceed

the total number of books published in Irish during
the last twenty years'. In 1968, according to the list
of publications issued by the National Library, 16
books in Irish classified as literature were published:
7 books of verse, 5 novels and 4 plays. That may be
taken to be a fair picture of the average annual output and, when we remember that much of it is
inevitably of purely ephemeral interest, it is not at
first sight very impressive.

By Irish standards, however, these figures are
reasonable, for there is very little publishing of any
kind. Iceland may have a population less than that
of Co. Cork, but the whole of Ireland, north and
south, publishes considerably fewer new titles in
English and Irish put together than Iceland's 600 or
so per annum! There are obvious historical and
political reasons for this extraordinary situation. As
we saw, the speakers of Irish remained untouched
by the cultural revolution which the invention of the
printing press brought about in the sixteenth century,
and remained dominated by an oral culture. The
English-speaking ascendancy which ruled the country
from the beginning of the seventeenth century was
consciously colonialist and looked to London; publishing in English flourished in Dublin for a time in
the eighteenth century, but only because the separate
legal systems of the two countries made the pirating
of English publications profitable, and it collapsed
when the English copyright law could be enforced

after the Act of Union in 1800. The shift from Irish
to English as the majority language brought about
no real change of attitude towards reading. English
became the medium through which a man dealt
with authority, and transacted business. It was read
in a few restricted fields—newspapers, political
pamphlets and religious tracts, for example—but
that was all; the patriotic ballads of the nineteenth
century continued the oral tradition in a new
language. The remarkable flowering of Anglo-Irish
literature in the early years of this century made no
impression on the broad masses of the Irish people,
and nearly all of it was published in London. Ireland
was a country where books were little read, except
for passing examinations, and where conversational
brilliance was more highly esteemed than breadth
of reading.

Anglo-Irish literature, whatever its origins, was
by its choice of language directed to a world audience.
Irish literature could be addressed only to Irishmen,
and, in the first place, to those whose native language
was Irish. As we have seen, these communities were
even more firmly rooted in their oral culture than
was the rest of the country; to have converted them
to a culture based on reading would have been a
formidable task, and it was not seriously attempted.
The problem is not peculiar to Ireland: Professor
Derick Thomson, speaking of the Scottish highlands
and islands, has said that the majority of Gaelic

speakers there regard the use of Gaelic for purposes other than everyday conversation as 'affected, or eccentric, or pertaining to a new and odd class, that of the language revivers', and it would be easy to cite examples from other areas, such as southern France, where the activities of the poets of the *Félibrige* are looked on with suspicion and scepticism by Provençal-speaking peasants. Máirtín Ó Cadhain claimed that his novel *Cré na Cille* had penetrated into houses where no other book had ever been bought except an almanac showing the dates of fairs and an occasional religious journal, and this solitary break-through is an eloquent illustration of the general failure of the new literature to speak to those who were its primary concern. As things stand, the reading public for modern Irish literature is a largely urban intelligentsia, some of whom are native speakers living in the towns, but of whom the largest proportion have learned the language. They live and work in a country which is overwhelmingly English-speaking, and indifferent to Irish; there is an obvious danger of such an intelligentsia degenerating into a complacent and inward-looking clique.

It is not easy to say what the potential size of that reading public is, but it might be estimated at about 400,000, which is roughly twice the population of Iceland, but only 10% of the population of Ireland, north and south. It probably, however, represents more people than were able to read Irish at any previous period in the country's history and that is a very encouraging reflection. But there are also disturbing features. The estimate of 400,000 people capable of reading Irish must be compared to a census figure of well over 600,000 native speakers of the language at the time of the foundation of the Gaelic League in 1893; all but a handful of those were illiterate in their own language, but they constituted a community from which a literature might have grown. Today, of our 400,000 potential readers of Irish, not more than 50,000 are native speakers of Irish; to the remaining 350,000, Irish is a second language learned at school. The implications of this for the future of writing in Irish are all too clear. The peculiar triumph of the new literature has been precisely that it grew out of the speech of the people, and that learners who wished to take part in the movement could do so only at the price of acquiring near-native ability in the use of the language. The continual shrinking of the Irish-speaking areas, and the very real possibility that they will disappear completely in another generation or two engenders an unwelcome division of the mind in the writers; while striving to purify and extend their language, they are always conscious that it may soon be merely a subject for academic study. Thus Ó Direáin's fine poem of homage to J. M. Synge ends with the words:

My people's way of life is decaying,
The sea serves no longer as a wall,

> But until Coill Chuain comes to Inismeáin
> The words which you once collected
> Will still live in a foreign tongue.

This thought that what a seventeenth century poet described as 'a new England called Ireland' is the ultimate fate of the country lies heavy on our writers; Ó Cadhain said in his recent lecture:

> A dark cloud hangs over Irish again. A worse thing than lack of recognition at home and abroad weighs on the writer. It is hard for a man to give of his best in a language which seems likely to die before himself, if he lives a few years more: this despair engenders a desire to fight fiercely for the language. Neither despair or fighting is good for him as a writer . . .

If the Irish-speaking areas disappear, writing in Irish will vanish too, for writing in a language which no mother speaks to her child is either pious sentimentality or an act of faith—an act of faith such as kept Hebrew literature alive in the Diaspora. But who would have continued to write in Hebrew, if, having returned to Zion, the Jewish people had rejected their traditional tongue? The fate of Irish literature will be decided for ever in the next generation; whatever it may be, it is right that the effort of a devoted handful to continue a great tradition should not be forgotten.

SAOL AGUS CULTÚR IN ÉIRINN
IRISH LIFE AND CULTURE

The following booklets have been published
in this series:

14. The Irish Language
    by David Greene

15. Irish Folk Custom and Belief
    by Seán Ó Súilleabháin

16. The Irish Harp
    by Joan Rimmer

17. Eriugena
    by John J. O'Meara

18. Writing in Irish Today
    by David Greene

Special Series:

Early Christian Irish Art
    by Françoise Henry
    (available also in French under the title
    Art Irlandais. The translation from the
    French is by Máire MacDermott)

Irish High Crosses
    by Françoise Henry
    (available also in French under the title
    Croix Sculptées Irlandaises)